ASSESSING YOUR CHILD'S PROGRESS

Testing and assessment in the National Curriculum

Pupils between the ages of 7 and 11 (Years 3–6) cover Key Stage 2 of the National Curriculum. In May of their final year of Key Stage 2 (Year 6) all pupils take written National Tests (commonly known as SATs) in the three most important subjects: English, Mathematics and Science. Your child may already have taken some National Tests at the end of Key Stage 1 (Year 2). These will have been in number, shape and space, reading, writing, handwriting and spelling.

At the end of Key Stage 1, your child will have been awarded a National Curriculum level for each subject tested. When your child eventually takes the Key Stage 2 tests, he or she again will be awarded a level. On average, pupils are expected to advance one level for every two years they are at school. The target for pupils at the end of Key Stage 1 is Level 2. By the end of Key Stage 2, four years later, the target is Level 4. The table below will show you how your child should progress.

Assessing your child's progress throughout Key Stage 2 of the National Curriculum

The aim of the Letts Assessment books is to help you monitor your child's progress in English, Mathematics and Science throughout Key Stage 2. There are four books for each subject – one for each year, starting with 7–8 year olds. The questions in the books become progressively harder with each year, so that for 10–11 year olds, the questions will be at a level similar to the Key Stage 2 National Tests.

After completing a book, your child will have a score which you will be able to interpret using the progress indicator provided. This will give you a guide to the level at which your child is working.

ASSESSING YOUR CHILD'S PROGRESS

Using this book to assess your child's progress in English

This book contains four basic features:

Questions:	4 reading tests, based on the English magazine 4 writing tests 1 handwriting test 1 spelling test
Answers:	showing acceptable responses and marks
Note to Parent:	giving advice on what your child should be doing and how to help
Progress Chart:	showing you how to interpret your child's marks to arrive at a level

- The reading tests are based on the magazine at the back, which can be detached. Before starting a reading test, your child should spend some time reading the relevant section of the magazine.
- Your child should not attempt to do all the questions in the book in one go. Try tackling one test at a time or, for the longer reading tests, try ten questions at a time. If your child does not understand the Writing, Handwriting or Spelling Test, you should explain what has to be done. Avoid doing this for the Reading Tests, however – particularly when your child is working on the test. Encourage your child to continue the test and move on to the next question. Afterwards, it is most valuable to go over questions that caused problems.
- When your child has completed the questions, turn to the Answer section at the back of the book. Using the recommended answers, award your child the appropriate mark or marks for each question. In the margin of each question page, there are small boxes. These are divided in half with the marks available for that question at the bottom, and a blank at the top for you to fill in your child's score. Enter the total number of marks at the end of each test.
- Collate your child's marks on the grid on page 34. Then add them up. Once you have the total, turn to page 24 at the front of the Answer section and look at the Progress Chart to determine your child's level.
- Work through the answers with your child, using the Note to Parent to help give advice, correct mistakes and explain problems.

Equipment your child will need for this book

All your child needs are a pen or pencil for writing, and writing paper for the four writing tests (about two sheets for each test). Your child may also like to have a rubber for changing answers.

Instructions

There are four reading tests – one on each section of the magazine:

- How the Elephant Became
- The Elephant
- A History of the Earth in Two Pages
- Leonardo

You can do the reading tests in any order. Take as much time as you wish to read each section of the magazine.

In some questions you will have to put a ring round the right answer like this:

Monday is

a month of the year	the first day of the week
a day when all the shops close	the second day of the week

In other questions you will be asked to write longer answers using words and sentences.

If you find a question difficult, don't worry about it, go on to the next question. After you have finished the test, talk to your parents about that question.

How the Elephant Became

Please read 'How the Elephant Became' on pages 1–7 of your magazine. Then answer these questions about the story. You may look at the magazine as often as you wish.

About the story — Questions 1–7

1 What did the horses do when Bombo tried to be a horse?

1 Q1

- They ran about.
- They laughed.
- They chased him away.

2 When a pack of wolves appeared Bombo

1 Q2

- ran away to hide
- lay on his back with his legs in the air
- charged at them

3 What happens in the story? Put these events in the right order by numbering each line. The first one has been done for you.

6 Q3

__ Bombo waded out to a small island in the middle of the river.
__ All the animals rolled on their sides with laughter.
__ Bombo threw every tree into the river.
__ Buffalo charged past with his family.
__ The forest was on fire.
_1_ Bombo tried to be a horse.
__ Bombo loaded the animals onto his back.

MARKS

4 a Where did Bombo go after all the animals laughed at him?

.... 1 Q4a

b Why did he go there?

....

.... 1 Q4b

5 The writer says that the animals set up a "terrible roaring, wailing, crying, howling, moaning sound".

Why were the animals so upset?

....

.... 1 Q5

6 a What did Bombo think when he first saw the fire?

.... 1 Q6a

b What made him change his mind?

....

.... 1 Q6b

1
Q6c

c What did Bombo do as soon as he realised that his help was needed?

....

....

1
Q7a

7 a Who said "Keep ducking yourselves in the water"?

....

1
Q7b

b Why did he say this?

....

....

About the characters — Questions 8–9

3
Q8

8 Write **three** phrases or sentences that show that Bombo did not like the other animals laughing at him.

1...

2...

3...

9 Bombo found that his special characteristics helped him to save the other animals.

Find **four** ways Bombo used his different characteristics, or features, to save the other animals.

4 Q9

1 ....

2 ....

3 ....

4 ....

How the story is written — Questions 10–11

10 The writer describes the fire as being "like a terrific red wind" and "like a thundering roof".

What do these two phrases tell us about the fire?

3 Q10

....

....

....

11 Write **two** phrases from the story that show that the river was flowing very quickly and powerfully.

2 Q11

1 ....

2 ....

Your opinion

Questions 12–13

2
Q12

12 Did you like the kind of animal Bombo became? Yes/No
Give reasons for your answer.

....

....

2
Q13

13 Did you enjoy this story? Yes/No
Explain your reasons in the box below.

Total
32
How the Elephant Became

The Elephant

Now please read 'The Elephant' on pages 8–9 of your magazine. Then answer these questions about the passage. You may look at the magazine as often as you wish.

About the passage — Questions 1–7

1 Write the missing information on the blank line to complete these sentences.

2 Q1

a When the elephant is six years old it is ………… times its weight at birth.

b Ten years ago in Africa there were over ………… elephants.

2 Why do poachers kill elephants?

1 Q2

…………

3 Why was a world ban on the sale of ivory agreed?

1 Q3

…………

4 Name **two** countries where the Asian elephant can be found.

2 Q4

1 ………… 2 …………

5 The writer describes several differences in the physical appearance of the Asian and African elephant.

Write about these **physical** differences in the box below.

6
Q5

6 At the end of the passage, the writer says the reader "can be certain of one thing". What is that one thing?

....

....

1
Q6

7 a What are the "insulting" tasks the African elephant has been spared?

....

....

....

....

3
Q7a

b Why has the African elephant been spared these "insulting" tasks?

....

....

1 Q7b

Opinion Question 8

8 a By using the phrase "insulting tasks", what is the writer revealing about his own views?

....

....

1 Q8a

b Do you agree with the writer's view that the Asian elephant has been made to carry out insulting tasks? Yes/No
Give reasons for your answer in the box below.

2 Q8b

Total 20 The Elephant

A History of the Earth in Two Pages

Please read 'A History of the Earth in Two Pages' in your magazine. Answer these questions about the comic strip. You may look at the magazine as often as you wish.

About the comic strip — Questions 1–5

1 How old is the world?

Captain Eco says the world is about .... years old.

1 Q1

2 How long have people lived on Earth?

Captain Eco believes that people have lived on Earth for

.... years.

1 Q2

3 Captain Eco gives the children a number of facts.

Write down the facts he gives the children about:

a coal ....

....

b disease ....

....

c chemicals ....

....

3 Q3

4 What was the population of the world in 1850?

....

1 Q4

5 How many species of animal disappear every year?

....

1 Q5

Opinion Questions 6–9

6 Why do you think that Captain Eco calls the children "Earthlings"?

....

....

1 Q6

7 In the first cartoon Captain Eco exclaims, "Disappearing Dinosaurs! This is going to be harder than I thought..."

a What was Captain Eco going to find difficult?

....

1 Q7a

b Why was the use of the phrase "Disappearing Dinosaurs!" so effective?

....

....

2 Q7b

8 **a** The term "Homo Sapiens" is Latin.

What do these words mean in English?

1 Q8a

....

b Why did Captain Eco think the use of the term "Homo Sapiens" was amusing?

1 Q8b

....

....

....

9 Captain Eco expresses his opinions about the way in which people use the Earth.

Write down **two** opinions that Captain Eco gives about the way we treat the Earth.

2 Q9

1. ....

....

2. ....

....

Total 15 A History of the Earth

Leonardo

Now please read 'Leonardo' on page 12 of your magazine and answer these questions about the poem. You may look at the magazine as often as you wish.

About the poem — Questions 1–2

1 Where did Leonardo go during his morning walk?

.... 1 Q1

2 a Where did Leonardo take the birds after he bought them?

.... 1 Q2a

b Why do you think he took the birds to this place?

.... 1 Q2b

About the characters — Questions 3–4

3 The poet wrote: Never questioning
The fee,

a What does this phrase mean?

.... 1 Q3a

....

1 Q3b

b What does this suggest about Leonardo's character?

....

1 Q4

4 What did Leonardo give the birds?

....

How the poem is written — Questions 5–6

1 Q5

5 In the market Leonardo saw wild birds in cages.

What words or phrases does the poet use to suggest that the birds were not happy?

....

....

1 Q6a

6 a What were the birds' "prisons"?

....

1 Q6b

b What does the use of the word "prisons" suggest about the poet's own views?

....

....

Your opinion — Questions 7–8

7 The poet has arranged the lines of the poem in an unusual way.

What reasons might he have for doing this?

2 Q7

8 How do you feel about Leonardo's actions in this poem?

Write your views in the box below.

2 Q8

Total 13 Leonardo

QUESTIONS WRITING

Instructions

Ask your parent to read the notes on page 28 before you begin. You can do the writing tests in any order you choose but you should try to do all four. You should read the magazine carefully before you start any of the writing tests because all the writing tests draw on ideas from the magazine.

Spend about ten minutes planning your writing and no longer than an hour doing each test. Ask your parent for some writing paper.

When you have finished your writing, check these details:

- spelling and punctuation;
- could you have described the characters or information in more detail?
- is your beginning as good as you can make it?
- have you written a sensible ending?
- are the events (information) clear to another reader? (paragraphs might help)

WRITING

MARKS

Just like Bombo...

1 In 'How the Elephant Became', Bombo is very brave but also very shy.

Write a short story about a shy hero or heroine.

18
Q1

You might like to include in your story:

- why the person is shy;
- the problem the shy person helps to sort out;
- how the shy person becomes a hero or heroine;
- how the story ends.

Letts

Lost in Space

2 In 'A History of the Earth in Two Pages' Captain Eco takes Michelle and Clive on a trip into space. Imagine you are taken on a trip into space but end up getting lost.

18
Q2

Write a short story about being lost in space.

You might like to think about:

- how did you get lost in space?
- where did you travel to?
- what happened?
- who did you meet?
- how did you get back to Earth?
- how did the story end?

WRITING

MARKS

What a Wonderful World!

3 Write some advice for all young people about how to keep the world a wonderful place.

18
Q3

You might like to think about:

- caring for the environment (animals, trees, cars, litter, etc.);
- caring for other people (friendship, kindness, food for the hungry, looking after those who need help);
- any other ways of making the world a better place.

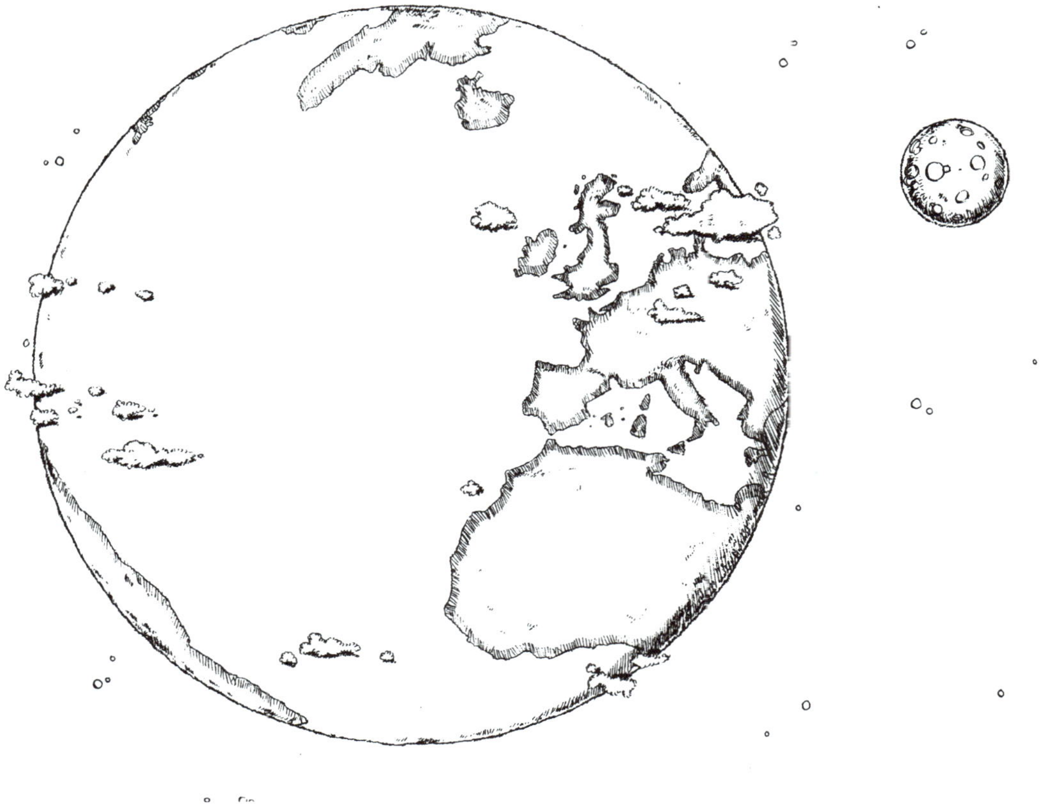

A Letter

4 Every year, elephants are killed by ivory poachers who sell the tusks to traders who use them to make ornaments.

18
Q4

Write a letter to a group of ivory poachers to try to persuade them not to kill the elephants.

Remember to say:

- why you are writing;
- why you think the elephants should not be killed;
- what the poachers should do.

(Remember you are trying to **persuade** this group of people.)

Photo: Gerald Cubitt (Bruce Coleman Ltd)

Handwriting test

Here is a short passage for you to copy out in your best handwriting. You may practise this passage as many times as you wish. Check that:

- you are forming all the letters correctly;
- your letters are the right size;
- you are joining your writing correctly;
- you try to join the letters of words smoothly.

Copy this passage:

At the water's edge,
The animals meet.
Elephant, zebra and buffalo too,
All drink peacefully,
While the fierce hippo just peeps
Above the waterline
As he keeps his quiet watch
Beside the water's edge.

Write the passage below.

....

....

....

....

....

....

....

....

Total

4

Handwriting

QUESTIONS SPELLING

Spelling test

Ask your parent to read out the story on page 33. The same story is written below, but it has some words missing. You should follow the story as your parent reads it the first time.

> Now your parent will read the story again. When you come to a blank line, wait for your mum or dad to tell you the missing word. Write the word on the line. If you are not sure how to spell it, just try to write the letters you think are correct.

Operation Noah

The Kariba Dam was .... nearly forty years ago. After the dam was ...., the waters of Lake Kariba .... a large .... where many wild animals lived. To save the animals, it was .... to mount one of the most .... animal rescues of this ....

The animals were .... on small .... in the newly formed lake .... they were unable to swim to safety. A small group of rangers .... that they would have to act .... if the animals

1 Q1
1 Q2
1 Q3
1 Q4
1 Q5
1 Q6
1 Q7
1 Q8
1 Q9
1 Q10
1 Q11
1 Q12

were not to .... Nearly five ....

animals were ...., put to sleep and taken by

.... or boats to safety. This ....

rescue became known as 'Operation Noah'.

Beside the .... waters of Lake Kariba it is hard

to .... what .... so long ago.

Without a ...., much is owed to the brave rangers

who .... fought to save so many animals.

Today, elephants, buffalo, zebra and many .... wild

animals .... to live along the banks of

Lake Kariba.

Operation Noah: rangers carry a waterbuck bull to safety

Photo: Jen and Des Bartlett (Bruce Coleman Ltd)

SPELLING

MARKS

Q13	1
Q14	1
Q15	1
Q16	1
Q17	1
Q18	1
Q19	1
Q20	1
Q21	1
Q22	1
Q23	1
Q24	1

Total
24
Spelling

Letts

MARKING YOUR CHILD'S QUESTIONS

- When marking your child's questions, remember that the answers given here are the answers the question-setter expects. You must look at your child's answers and judge whether they deserve credit.
- When you go through the questions with your child, try to be positive. Look for good things that have been done as well as discussing where errors have been made. When discussing your child's writing it is valuable to help your child re-draft what he or she has written but remember that re-drafting is mostly about improving the **structure** of the story and not just *"writing it out in best"*.
- Enter your child's marks on the grid on page 34, and then calculate your child's overall score. The table below will help you interpret your child's level for English.

Progress Chart

Total marks scored	Progress made	Suggested action
56 or below	Your child's mark shows that he or she is probably at an earlier stage of development and working at Level 3.	In reading, encourage your child to read a wide range of texts. Help him or her to infer meanings from texts and to develop writing by using more complex sentence structures.
57–75	A mark in this range indicates that your child is starting to develop some skills in reading and writing associated with Level 4.	In reading, help your child to develop skills of inference and deduction. In writing, focus on developing a suitable and clearly distinguished beginning, middle and ending.
76–99	Your child is consolidating his or her skills in reading and writing at Level 4.	In reading, help your child to locate and use ideas and information from a range of reading materials. In writing, encourage the use of more adventurous vocabulary.
100–119	A mark in this range indicates that your child is starting to move on to Level 5.	In reading, help extend your child's use of inference and deduction. Discuss key features of texts, themes and characters. In writing, help your child to organise sentences into paragraphs.
120–139	Your child is consolidating his or her skills in reading and writing at Level 5.	In reading, help your child to select relevant information to support his or her views about texts. Help your child to develop a more formal style of writing when appropriate, using accurate spelling and punctuation within sentences.
140 and above	Your child's mark shows that he or she is working at the top of Level 5 and might be ready to move on to Level 6.	In reading, encourage your child to retrieve and collate information from a range of sources, and to give personal responses to literature. In writing, help your child to adapt his or her style to write for different purposes.

- A child at the end of Year 6 (10–11 year olds) should be, of the above statements, at about the third statement in order to meet the national target level. If your child has scored 56–75 marks, you may find it useful to work through the 9–10 book in this series in order to help your child consolidate skills at Level 4.

ANSWERS

Narrative Reading: 'How the Elephant Became'

1	They laughed.		*1 mark*
2	lay on his back with his legs in the air		*1 mark*
3	4	Bombo waded out to a small island in the middle of the river.	*1 mark*
	3	All the animals rolled on their sides with laughter.	*1 mark*
	7	Bombo threw every tree into the river.	*1 mark*
	2	Buffalo charged past with his family.	*1 mark*
	5	The forest was on fire.	*1 mark*
	1	Bombo tried to be a horse.	
	6	Bombo loaded the animals onto his back.	*1 mark*
4	a	to a small island in the middle of the river	*1 mark*
	b	Answers should indicate that Bombo wanted to be alone, unseen.	*1 mark*
5	because they were trapped between the fire and the river		*1 mark*
6	a	he thought that it was a fine sight	*1 mark*
	b	he heard the animals and became aware of their distress	*1 mark*
	c	he crossed the river, picked up the animals and brought them to safety	*1 mark*
7	a	Lion	*1 mark*
	b	so that the animals would have wet fur and not get burned	*1 mark*

8
- Bombo stared at them in horror
- But Bombo just stood
- This was much worse than imitating some other animal
- pretended to be inspecting one of his feet, as if he were alone
- letting the tears trickle down his long nose
- he'd had enough
- from then on, Bombo lived alone

Any three answers: 1 mark each — *3 marks*

9
- he crossed the river with his big, strong legs
- Bombo carried creatures with hooves and big feet on his back
- with his long, silly nose he reached out and picked up the animals
- the little clinging things clung to the great folds of his ears
- he put his long silly tusks under the roots of the burning trees

Any four answers: 1 mark each — *4 marks*

10 Answers should indicate the following ideas: heat, sound, colour, speed, the fact that the fire was over the animals' heads.
Any three answers: 1 mark each — *3 marks*

11 There are many phrases in the story which indicate the river's speed and power, e.g. "the black river swirled and rumbled".
Any two examples from the story: 1 mark each — *2 marks*

12 Accept any reasons which explain the Yes/No response, e.g. "I liked Bombo" is not acceptable but "I liked Bombo because he was brave" would be sufficient.
Up to two reasons: 1 mark each — *2 marks*

13 Accept any reason which explains the Yes/No response.
Up to two reasons: 1 mark each — *2 marks*

Total: 32 marks

Note to parent

The questions at the beginning of 'How the Elephant Became' focus on skills which require your child to show an understanding of the main points of the story. These are skills associated with Level 3. Harder questions have required your child to show an understanding of significant events and characters and to start to use inference and deduction. These are skills that are associated with Level 4.

Towards the end of the test your child is also asked to select or interpret sentences and phrases from the text in order to answer questions. These are skills associated with Level 5.

Non-narrative Reading: 'The Elephant'

1 a ten — *1 mark*

b a million — *1 mark*

2 for their ivory tusks — *1 mark*

3 because the number of elephants fell so low — *1 mark*

4
- India
- Sri Lanka
- Malaysia
- China
- Indonesia

Any two countries: 1 mark each — *2 marks*

5 Accept only the following **physical** differences:

Asian elephant	**African elephant**
forehead domed	forehead flat
head is carried low	head carried higher
back humped	back has slight dip
ears smaller	ears larger (for cooling the body)
tusks smaller	tusks larger
smaller in size	larger in size

Up to six differences: 1 mark each — *6 marks*

6 that by the time the passage is read there will be fewer elephants in the world — *1 mark*

7 a Accept any of the following:
- clearing forests
- taking part in ceremonial parades
- being used for warfare
- carrying heavy things or burdens
- being used as a circus performer

Award 1 mark for one reason, 2 marks for two or three reasons, 3 marks for four or five reasons. — *3 marks*

b the African elephant is much more difficult to control — *1 mark*

8 a Accept answers that reflect that the writer thinks the tasks that the Asian elephant has had to do are degrading. — *1 mark*

b Accept any reasons that explain the Yes/No response, e.g. "I agree with the writer" is not sufficient but "I agree with the writer because I think elephants should not be tamed" is acceptable.
Up to two reasons: 1 mark each — *2 marks*

Total: 20 marks

Note to parent

The questions at the beginning of 'The Elephant' require your child to show an understanding of the main points of the passage. Harder questions ask your child to identify differences and to infer and deduce meaning from the text. If your child has had difficulty in answering questions requiring inference and deduction, discuss the relevant part of the text. Help your child to see the implied meaning within the text.

Non-narrative Reading: 'A History of the Earth in Two Pages'

1 five billion — *1 mark*

2 one hundred thousand — *1 mark*

3 a we've used as much coal in the last 50 years as in the whole of history to date — *1 mark*

b 40,000 children die each day of diseases that are preventable — *1 mark*

c 70,000 new chemicals have been released into the environment in the last 150 years — *1 mark*

4 1 billion — *1 mark*

5 over 170,000 — *1 mark*

6 Accept answers which reflect the understanding that the children live on Earth. — *1 mark*

7 a teaching Michelle and Clive about the Earth's problems — *1 mark*

b Credit answers which relate to:
- sound – the play on "d"
- the dinosaurs have disappeared from the Earth's environment (humans might disappear too)

Up to two reasons: 1 mark each — *2 marks*

8 a wise man — *1 mark*

b Credit answers which reflect that Captain Eco believed that people on Earth had been anything but wise in managing the Earth. — *1 mark*

9 Accept answers which reflect the following ideas:
- what's the point of getting richer if you're killing the planet?
- if you destroy these things you destroy yourselves
- it can't last... you'd be nowhere without the Earth's resources

Any two answers: 1 mark each — *2 marks*

Total: 15 marks

Note to parent

The questions at the beginning of this test ask your child to identify facts from the text. Harder questions ask your child to identify opinions within a text that has many facts. Your child is also asked to comment on the effectiveness of some of the language used. These higher order skills are associated with Level 5.

Poetry: 'Leonardo'

1 to the market (Market Street) — *1 mark*

2 a to a tree on top of a hill — *1 mark*

b to set them free — *1 mark*

3	a	he did not care about the price	*1 mark*
	b	he was unconcerned about money, or he was generous	*1 mark*
4	their freedom		*1 mark*
5	Silent in the dust, the heat.		*1 mark*
6	a	their cages	*1 mark*
	b	Credit answers that indicate that the poet does not agree with wild birds being held captive.	*1 mark*
7	Accept any reason which reflects an appreciation of the line layout. Answers may include reference to using language effectively, or that the layout suggests the shape of wings, flight, etc. *Up to two reasons: 1 mark each*		*2 marks*
8	Accept any reasons which are explained, e.g. "I think Leonardo is right" is not acceptable but "I think Leonardo is right because it is cruel to keep birds in cages" is sufficient. *Up to two reasons: 1 mark each*		*2 marks*
			Total: 13 marks

Note to parent

Many of the questions in this test are challenging because they relate to abstract ideas such as freedom. If your child has difficulty with this test you might wish to discuss some of the issues the poem raises, e.g. keeping wild animals in cages, freedom, captivity and the character of Leonardo as inferred in this poem. After discussing the issues, let your child try the questions again.

Notes for parents on the writing tests

The National Curriculum places importance on children having a range of writing experiences. Your child should try all four tests but they can be tried in any order.

Each starting point suggests ideas or information that your child might wish to include in his or her writing. Before your child begins, he or she should spend a little time planning (about ten minutes). You may wish to help with this either by reading the starting points through, or by discussing what he or she might write. By helping to plan the organisation of your child's writing, you will help him or her to develop writing skills. The marking keys can also guide you to help your child, by showing how writing skills should develop between levels.

Make sure your child has about two sheets of writing paper for each test. Your child should spend no longer than one hour doing each test.

Marking keys

Use the marking keys on pages 29–30 to make a decision about your child's writing level in each piece of writing. Use the first key to mark 'Just like Bombo…' and 'Lost in Space'; use the second key to mark 'What a Wonderful World!' and 'A Letter'. Turn to page 31 to find out how to award marks using each key.

Marking key – stories

	How is the story written and organised?	Q1 Yes	Q1 No	Q2 Yes	Q2 No
LEVEL 4	Does the story have a suitable opening?	☐	☐	☐	☐
	Does the story have a clear beginning, middle and end?	☐	☐	☐	☐
	Are the events of the story sensibly related?	☐	☐	☐	☐
	Does the ending relate convincingly to the main events (e.g. not just "we all went home")?	☐	☐	☐	☐
	Is the vocabulary interesting and lively?	☐	☐	☐	☐
	Are complex sentences used (e.g. phrases joined by "so that", "although", "if")?	☐	☐	☐	☐
	Are descriptive phrases used (e.g. "as fast as his legs could carry him")?	☐	☐	☐	☐
	Overall, is the writing interesting?	☐	☐	☐	☐
LEVEL 5	Is the writing well organised and well paced overall?	☐	☐	☐	☐
	Are there any interesting story devices, for example:				
	• does it start with dialogue?	☐	☐	☐	☐
	• does it start in the middle of a dramatic event?	☐	☐	☐	☐
	• does it move between times and places?	☐	☐	☐	☐
	• does it include a sub-plot?	☐	☐	☐	☐
	• does it end with a twist in the story?	☐	☐	☐	☐
	Are events, dialogue and description skilfully interwoven?	☐	☐	☐	☐
	Does the writer express personal point of view, for example by:				
	• commenting on characters and events?	☐	☐	☐	☐
	• giving an idea of characters' thoughts and feelings?	☐	☐	☐	☐
	Does the ending relate convincingly to the central plot?	☐	☐	☐	☐
	Is the language vivid and interesting?	☐	☐	☐	☐
	Is there a mixture of simple and complex sentences?	☐	☐	☐	☐
	Is the reader's interest engaged and sustained?	☐	☐	☐	☐

	How is the story presented?	Q1 Yes	Q1 No	Q2 Yes	Q2 No
LEVEL 4	Are capital letters, full stops and question marks used correctly in most cases?	☐	☐	☐	☐
	Is there punctuation within sentences (e.g. commas, speech marks, apostrophes)?	☐	☐	☐	☐
	Are most regular long words spelt correctly (e.g. "condition", "finally")?	☐	☐	☐	☐
	Is the handwriting joined and clear?	☐	☐	☐	☐
	Are paragraphs used in some instances?	☐	☐	☐	☐
LEVEL 5	Are capital letters, full stops and question marks used correctly in almost all cases?	☐	☐	☐	☐
	Is punctuation within sentences (e.g. commas, apostrophes, speech marks) used correctly in most cases?	☐	☐	☐	☐
	Are most long words spelt correctly, including words with complex regular patterns (e.g. "satisfied", " apprehensive")?	☐	☐	☐	☐
	Is the handwriting joined, clear and fluent?	☐	☐	☐	☐
	Are paragraphs used to separate the beginning, middle and end of the piece?	☐	☐	☐	☐

Marking key – information writing

	How is the writing organised?	Q3 Yes	Q3 No	Q4 Yes	Q4 No
LEVEL 4	Does the writing have a suitable introduction/opening?	☐	☐	☐	☐
	Is the information presented in a way that a reader can follow?	☐	☐	☐	☐
	Are suitable formats used (e.g. "Dear...," for a letter)?	☐	☐	☐	☐
	Are the main points/aspects of information covered?	☐	☐	☐	☐
	Is there a reasonable amount of detail?	☐	☐	☐	☐
	Is there a suitable final sentence?	☐	☐	☐	☐
	Is the vocabulary precise and varied (with suitable technical words used)?	☐	☐	☐	☐
	Are complex sentences used (e.g. phrases joined by "so that", "although", "if")?	☐	☐	☐	☐
	Are phrases used to clarify meaning (e.g. "with an emblem on top")?	☐	☐	☐	☐
	Overall, is the writing interesting?	☐	☐	☐	☐
LEVEL 5	Is the writing organised and well paced overall?	☐	☐	☐	☐
	Does the opening make clear the purpose of the writing?	☐	☐	☐	☐
	Is the reader's interest engaged and sustained?	☐	☐	☐	☐
	Is the language precise, using technical and specific words where needed?	☐	☐	☐	☐
	Is there a mixture of simple and complex sentences?	☐	☐	☐	☐
	Are the main issues covered?	☐	☐	☐	☐
	Are individual points adequately covered?	☐	☐	☐	☐
	Are individual points sensibly organised and linked?	☐	☐	☐	☐

	How is the writing presented?	Q3 Yes	Q3 No	Q4 Yes	Q4 No
LEVEL 4	Are capital letters, full stops and question marks used correctly in most cases?	☐	☐	☐	☐
	Is there punctuation within sentences (e.g. commas, speech marks, apostrophes)?	☐	☐	☐	☐
	Are most regular long words spelt correctly (e.g. "condition", "finally")?	☐	☐	☐	☐
	Is the handwriting joined and clear?	☐	☐	☐	☐
	Are paragraphs used in some instances?	☐	☐	☐	☐
LEVEL 5	Are capital letters, full stops and question marks used correctly in almost all cases?	☐	☐	☐	☐
	Is punctuation within sentences (e.g. commas, apostrophes, speech marks) used correctly in most cases?	☐	☐	☐	☐
	Are most long words spelt correctly, including words with complex regular patterns (e.g. "satisfied", "apprehensive")?	☐	☐	☐	☐
	Is the handwriting joined, clear and fluent?	☐	☐	☐	☐
	Are paragraphs used to separate the beginning, middle and end of the piece?	☐	☐	☐	☐

Deciding the level of attainment:

For each piece of writing, follow the steps below.

Using the keys provided, decide which level best describes your child's writing in a particular test. Award marks from the range given according to how well you feel your child's writing meets the criteria. Fill in the marks on the marking grid on page 34.

1 Start with the questions for Level 4.

- where you are able to answer yes to only one or two questions your child is probably at an earlier stage of development and working at Level 3;

  (award 4 marks)

- where you are able to answer yes to about half the questions your child is starting to move on from Level 3 and is working towards Level 4;

  (award 5–7 marks)

- where you are able to answer yes to most of the questions your child is working well within Level 4 (particularly if this happens on all the writing tests);

  (award 8–10 marks)

- where you are able to answer yes to all the questions at Level 4, go on to consider the Level 5 questions.

2 Using the Level 5 questions:

- if you are able to respond yes to only one or two questions for Level 5 then your child is working mainly in the area of Level 4;

  (award 10 marks)

- where you are able to answer yes to about half the questions your child is starting to move on from Level 4 and is working towards Level 5;

  (award 11–13 marks)

- where you are able to answer yes to most of the questions, your child is working well within Level 5;

  (award 14–16 marks)

- where you are able to answer yes to all the questions, your child is working at the top end of Level 5 and may be ready to move on to tackle work that will lead to Level 6 (particularly if this happens on all the writing tests).

  (award 17–18 marks)

A parent's guide to the handwriting test

The handwriting test consists of one passage that your child should copy out in his or her best handwriting. Your child may practise the test or words from it as often as is helpful. The emphasis of the test is on:

- correct letter formation;
- correct size of letters ;
- joining letters correctly;
- the development of a fluent style.

Note to parent

At Level 2 letters should be correctly formed and consistent in size. At Level 3 handwriting should be joined and legible. At Levels 4 and 5 it is important that the handwriting style has developed so that it is fluent, joined, legible and clear. Schools choose the handwriting style that they will teach and a number of different styles are available. Some handwriting styles are fully joined, such as cursive. Other styles, such as italic, do not have all letters joined. In such cases, the handwriting style allows for most letters to join and there are consistent rules about joins. You may wish to find out which handwriting style your child is taught so that you can make a judgement about joins.

The handwriting test should be scored as follows:

All letters are formed correctly and are the correct size.	*1 mark*
The handwriting is joined correctly.	*1 mark*
The passage is written in a legible, joined style.	*1 mark*
The handwriting style is fluent; letters flow easily into one another and joins are even.	*1 mark*

Total: 4 marks

In this example, the letter 'k' is a little too large and the letter size is sometimes inconsistent (e.g. in the word 'drink'). The handwriting is joined correctly (1 mark) and is written in a legible, joined style (1 mark). Although the handwriting is *becoming* fluent, some of the joins (e.g. in the word 'quiet') do not flow evenly (Total: 2 marks):

All drink peacefully,
While the fierce hippo just peeps
Above the waterline
As he Keeps his quiet watch

This example shows handwriting which is fluent, joined, legible and clear (Total: 4 marks):

All drink peacefully,
While the fierce hippo just peeps
Above the waterline
As he keeps his quiet watch

A parent's guide to the spelling test

Your child's version of the spelling test is printed on pages 22–23. This test consists of a short story with blank spaces which have to be filled with the spelling test words. The story is written out in full for you below and you can detach it if you wish.

Read the text of the story out loud to your child **twice**. The first time read it through without stopping so that your child gets the sense of the story. Then read it a second time, pausing where your child has to write in the missing words in his or her version of the story.

In your text, the words printed in bold italics are the words your child will have to spell.

Spelling test – for parents to read aloud

Operation Noah

The Kariba Dam was ***built*** nearly forty years ago. After the dam was ***completed***, the waters of Lake Kariba ***filled*** a large ***valley*** where many wild animals lived. To save the animals, it was ***necessary*** to mount one of the most ***remarkable*** animal rescues of this ***century***.

The animals were ***trapped*** on small ***islands*** in the newly formed lake ***because*** they were unable to swim to safety. A small group of rangers ***decided*** that they would have to act ***immediately*** if the animals were not to ***drown***. Nearly five ***thousand*** animals were ***captured***, put to sleep and taken by ***trucks*** or boats to safety. This ***tremendous*** rescue became known as 'Operation Noah'.

Beside the ***peaceful*** waters of Lake Kariba it is hard to ***imagine*** what ***occurred*** so long ago. Without a ***doubt***, much is owed to the brave rangers who ***successfully*** fought to save so many animals. Today, elephants, buffalo, zebra and many ***other*** wild animals ***continue*** to live along the banks of Lake Kariba.

Spelling test answers – parent's marking guide

1 built
2 completed
3 filled
4 valley
5 necessary
6 remarkable
7 century
8 trapped
9 islands
10 because
11 decided
12 immediately
13 drown
14 thousand
15 captured
16 trucks
17 tremendous
18 peaceful
19 imagine
20 occurred
21 doubt
22 successfully
23 other
24 continue

The score from the spelling test is converted into marks which contribute to the overall level for writing. Marks should be given as follows:

Number of correct words	Marks
1–6	1
7–12	2
13–18	3
19–24	4

Note to parent

The marks from this test should be transferred to the marking grid overleaf.

MARKING GRID

READING ***Pages 2–15***

Test	Marks available	Marks scored
'How the Elephant Became'	32	
'The Elephant'	20	
'A History of the Earth in Two Pages'	15	
'Leonardo'	13	
Total	**80**	

WRITING ***Pages 17–23***

Test	Marks available	Marks scored
Just like Bombo…	18	
Lost in Space	18	
What a Wonderful World!	18	
A Letter	18	
Handwriting (see page 32)	**4**	
Spelling (see overleaf)	**4**	
Total	**80**	

TO CALCULATE AN OVERALL ENGLISH SCORE

Before calculating an overall score for English, work out your child's level of attainment in Reading and Writing separately. Determining these levels separately will allow you to identify your child's particular strengths and weaknesses in English. Record your child's scores in each test in the grids provided.

Determining a level for Reading

Below Level 4	Level 4	Level 5	Level 5+
0–28	29–53	54–69	70–80

Determining a level for Writing

Below Level 4	Level 4	Level 5	Level 5+
0–28	29–53	54–69	70–80

When all the tests have been completed you will be able to work out the overall total for English.

Totals	Marks available	Marks scored
Reading total	80	
Writing total	80	
Total for English	**160**	

Use the progress chart on page 24 to determine your child's level in English. The chart also suggests ways for you to help improve your child's reading and writing.

How the Elephant Became

by Ted Hughes

Long ago when the world was brand new, before animals or birds, the sun rose into the sky and brought the first day.

To begin with, all the creatures were pretty much alike – very different from what they are now. They had no idea what they were going to become. Some wanted to become linnets, some wanted to become lions, some wanted to become other things. The ones that wanted to become lions practised at being lions – and by and by, sure enough, they began to turn into lions. So, the ones that wanted to become linnets practised at being linnets, and slowly they turned into linnets. And so on.

But there were other creatures that came about in other ways...

The unhappiest of all the creatures was Bombo. Bombo didn't know what to become. At one time he thought he might make a fairly good horse. At another time he thought that perhaps he was meant to be a kind of bull. But it was no good. Not only the horses, but all the other creatures too, gathered to laugh at him when he tried to be a horse. And when he tried to be a bull, the bulls just walked away shaking their heads.

"Be yourself," they all said.

Bombo sighed. That's all he ever heard: "Be yourself. Be yourself." What was himself? That's what he wanted to know.

So most of the time he just stood, with sad eyes, letting the wind blow his ears this way and that, while the other creatures raced around him and above him, perfecting themselves.

"I'm just stupid," he said to himself. "Just stupid and slow and I shall never become anything."

That was his main trouble, he felt sure. He was much too slow and clumsy – and so big! None of the other creatures were anywhere near so big. He searched hard to find another creature as big as he was, but there was not one. This made him feel all the more silly and in the way.

But this was not all. He had great ears that flapped and hung, and a long, long nose. His nose was useful. He could pick things up with it. But none of the other creatures had a nose anything like it. They all had small neat noses, and they laughed at his. In fact, with that, and his ears, and his long white sticking-out tusks, he was a sight.

As he stood, there was a sudden thunder of hooves. Bombo looked up in alarm.

“Aside, aside, aside!” roared a huge voice. “We're going down to drink.”

Bombo managed to force his way backwards into a painful clump of thorn-bushes, just in time to let Buffalo charge past with all his family. Their long black bodies shone, their curved horns tossed, their tails screwed and curled, as they pounded down towards the water in a cloud of dust. The earth shook under them.

“There's no doubt,” said Bombo, “who they are. If only I could be as sure of what I am as Buffalo is of what he is.”

Then he pulled himself together.

“To be myself,” he said aloud, “I shall have to do something that no other creature does. Lion roars and pounces, and Buffalo charges up and down bellowing. Each of these creatures does something that no other creature does. So. What shall I do?”

He thought hard for a minute.

Then he lay down, rolled over on to his back, and waved his four great legs in the air. After that he stood on his head and lifted his hind legs straight up as if he were going to sunburn the soles of his feet. From this position, he lowered himself back on to his four feet, stood up and looked round. The others should soon get to know me by that, he thought.

Nobody was in sight, so he waited until a pack of wolves appeared on the horizon. Then he began again. On to his back, his legs in the air, then on to his head, and his hind legs straight up.

"Phew!" he grunted, as he lowered himself. "I shall need some practice before I can keep this up for long."

When he stood up and looked round him this second time, he got a shock. All the animals were round him in a ring, rolling on their sides with laughter.

"Do it again! Oh, do it again!" they were crying, as they rolled and laughed. "Do it again. Oh, I shall die with laughter. Oh, my sides, my sides!"

Bombo stared at them in horror.

After a few minutes the laughter died down.

"Come on!" roared Lion. "Do it again and make us laugh. You look so silly when you do it."

But Bombo just stood. This was much worse than imitating some other animal. He had never made them laugh so much before.

He sat down and pretended to be inspecting one of his feet, as if he were alone. And, one by one, now that there was nothing to laugh at, the other animals walked away, still chuckling over what they had seen.

"Next show same time tomorrow!" shouted Fox, and they all burst out laughing again.

Bombo sat, playing with his foot, letting the tears trickle down his long nose.

Well, he'd had enough. He'd tried to be himself, and all the animals had laughed at him.

That night he waded out to a small island in the middle of the great river that ran through the forest. And there, from then on, Bombo lived alone, seen by nobody but the little birds and a few beetles.

One night, many years later, Parrot suddenly screamed and flew up into the air above the trees. All his feathers were singed. The forest was on fire.

Within a few minutes, the animals were running for their lives. Jaguar, Wolf, Stag, Cow, Bear, Sheep, Cockerel, Mouse, Giraffe – all were running side by side and jumping over each other to get away from the flames. Behind them, the fire came through the tree-tops like a terrific red wind.

"Oh dear! Oh dear! Our houses, our children!" cried the animals.

On and on they ran, hour after hour, and all they could hear was the thunder of the fire at their tails.

On into the middle of the next day, and still they were running.

At last they came to the wide, deep, swift river. They could go no further. Behind them the fire boomed as it leapt from tree to tree.

They all set up a terrible roaring, wailing, crying, howling, moaning sound. It seemed like the end of the animals. The fire came nearer, bending over them like a thundering roof, while the black river swirled and rumbled beside them.

Out on his island stood Bombo, admiring the fire which made a fine sight through the smoke with its high spikes of red flame. He knew he was quite safe on his island. The fire couldn't cross that great stretch of water very easily.

At first he didn't see the animals crowding low by the edge of the water. The smoke and ash were too thick in the air. But soon he heard them. He recognised Lion's voice shouting:

"Keep ducking yourselves in the water. Keep your fur wet and the sparks will not burn you."

And the voice of Sheep crying:

"If we duck ourselves we're swept away by the river."

And the other creatures – Gnu, Ferret, Cobra, Partridge, crying:

"We must drown or burn. Goodbye, brothers and sisters!"

It certainly did seem like the end of the animals.

Without a pause, Bombo pushed his way into the water. The river was deep, the current heavy and fierce, but Bombo's legs were both long and strong. Burnt trees, that had fallen into the river higher up and were drifting down, banged against him, but he hardly felt them.

In a few minutes he was coming up into shallow water towards the animals. He was almost too late. The flames were forcing them, step by step, into the river, where the current was snatching them away.

When the animals saw Bombo looming through the smoke, a great shout went up:

"It's Bombo! It's Bombo!"

All the animals took up the cry:

"Bombo! Bombo!"

Bombo kept coming closer. As he came, he sucked up water in his long silly nose and squirted it over his back, to protect himself from the heat and the sparks. Then, with the same long, silly nose he reached out and began to pick up the animals, one by one, and seat them on his back.

"Take us!" cried Mole.

"Take us!" cried Monkey.

He loaded his back with the creatures that had hooves and big feet; then he told the little clinging things to cling on to the great folds of his ears. Soon he had every single creature aboard. Then he turned and began to wade back across the river, carrying all the animals of the forest towards safety.

Once they were safe on the island they danced for joy. Then they sat down to watch the fire. Suddenly Mouse gave a shout:

"Look! The wind is bringing sparks across the river. The sparks are blowing into the island trees. We shall burn here too."

As he spoke, one of the trees on the edge of the island crackled into flame. The animals set up a great cry and began to run in all directions.

"Help! Help! Help! We shall burn here too!"

But Bombo was ready. He put those long silly tusks of his, that he had once been so ashamed of, under the roots of the burning tree and heaved it into the river. He threw every tree into the river till the island was bare. The sparks now fell on to the bare torn ground, where the animals trod them out easily. Bombo had saved them again.

Next morning the fire had died out at the river's edge. The animals on the island looked across at the smoking, blackened plain where the forest had been. Then they looked round for Bombo.

He was nowhere to be seen.

"Bombo!" they shouted. "Bombo!" And listened to the echo.

But he had gone.

He is still very hard to find. Though he is huge and strong, he is very quiet.

The Elephant

by Desmond Morris

After it is born the young elephant grows very fast. It feeds on its mother's milk for over three years, sucking the liquid not with its trunk but with its mouth. Once it is weaned it will never again take food directly into its mouth in this way. It will always use its trunk first and then transfer the food to its mouth.

By the time it is six years old the young elephant will weigh ten times as much as it did at birth. Four years later it will start breeding itself. If it is a female it will produce a new calf every three years until it dies or is too old to breed. A few elephants manage to live almost as long as man, but most will be lucky to get past thirty years of age.

In Africa, just over ten years ago, there were over a million elephants. Since then poachers have killed half of them. All that these men wanted was the ivory. The rest of the dead elephant was left untouched where it fell. They stole the great curved tusks and smuggled them to the Far East where carvers shaped them into expensive ornaments. The ivory traders grew rich caring little for the fate of the elephants just so long as there were more in Africa waiting to be killed.

Eventually the numbers fell so low that a world ban on the sale of ivory was agreed. This helped a little, but the more daring poachers still attacked at night and continued to rob Africa of its greatest animal.

Asian elephants survive in small, remote areas of the forests of India and Sri Lanka, through Indochina, Malaysia and southern China, down into parts of Indonesia.

The Asian and the African are the only two kinds of elephants left alive today. They are very similar, but differ in several details. The Asian has a domed forehead, the African's is flat. The Asian carries its head low and has a humped back; the African carries its head higher and has a slight dip in the middle of its back. The ears of the Asian elephant are smaller than those of the African. (This is because an elephant's ears are used for cooling the body and the African suffers more from the heat than the Asian.) The tusks of the female Asian elephant are so small they cannot be seen outside its mouth; the tusks of the female African elephant, although smaller than those of the male, are clearly visible at a distance. The Asian elephant is slightly smaller than the African and it is also easier to tame. Asian elephants have been used from ancient times for clearing forests, for ceremonial parades, for warfare, as beasts of burden and as circus performers. Being much more difficult to control, the African elephant has been spared these insulting tasks.

Asian elephant

African elephant

By the time you read these words, you can be certain of one thing – there will already be far fewer elephants in the world. After millions of years, the era of these animal giants is drawing to a close. We have been very lucky to be alive while they are still with us, to marvel at them and enjoy their company.

Text adapted and reproduced from *The World of Animals* by Desmond Morris, published by Jonathan Cape. Photo of Asian elephant: Michael Freeman (Bruce Coleman Ltd); photo of African elephant: Mark N. Boulton (Bruce Coleman Ltd).

MEANWHILE...

Captain Eco takes the Earthlings Clive and Michelle into space. He has a lesson or two to teach them about the Earth.

A HISTORY OF THE EARTH

IN TWO PAGES

Reproduced from *Captain Eco and the Fate of the Earth* by Jonathon Porritt, illustrations by Ellis Nadler, published by Dorling Kindersley.

Leonardo

Leonardo, painter, taking
Morning air
On Market Street
Saw the wild birds in their cages
Silent in
The dust, the heat.

Took his purse from out his pocket
Never questioning
The fee,
Bore the cages to the green shade
Of a hill-top
Cypress tree.

"What you lost," said Leonardo,
"I now give to you
Again,
Free as noon and night and morning,
As the sunshine,
As the rain."

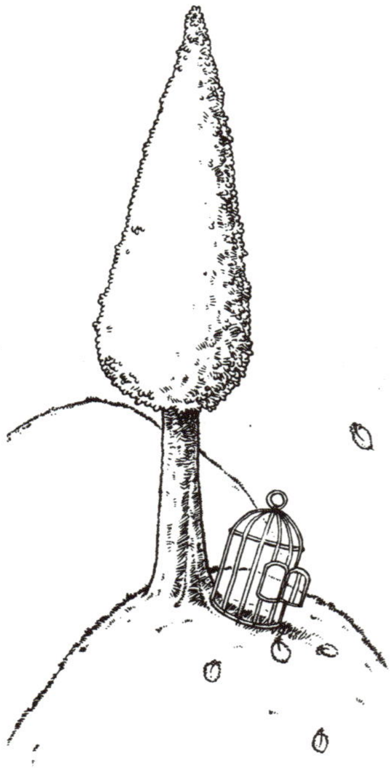

And he took them from their prisons,
Held them to
The air, the sky;
Pointed them to the bright heaven.
"Fly!" said Leonardo.
"Fly!"

by Charles Causley

'Leonardo' reprinted from *Collected Poems* by Charles Causley, published by Macmillan.